Reaching Answers

EVANGELIST MADORA D BOND

Reaching Answers

Copyright © 2024 by Evangelist Madora D. Bond

All Rights Reserved. No part of this publication may be reproduced, stored in a retrieval system, or transmitted, in any form or by any means, electronic, mechanical, photocopying, recording, or otherwise, without the written permission of the author.

Cover design by: Creative Solutionss

Published by: Evangelist Madora D Bond

Other books by the Publisher.

Do You Really See Momma Now – Copyright 2024

Rest in Him – Copyright 2022

Bye, Revealed Essence – Copyright 2018

Faithful Depths

Keys are in many fashions. They grant access; they prohibit entry. You must know how to use those within your grasp.

Dedication

This publication is to continuously encourage seeking enlightened understanding of the Word of God covered by the blood of His only begotten son, Jesus Christ.

> *Looking unto Jesus the author and finisher of **our** faith; who for the joy that was set before him endured the cross, despising the shame, and is set down at the right hand of the throne of God.*
> **Heb 12:2**

Wanting is not always the choice. Nevertheless, is an option too.

Preface

Herein lies a faith walk. A crooked path could be made straight and plain. You have an advocate.

> *"(For we walk by faith, not by sight:)"* **2 Cor 5:7**
>
> *Teach me thy way, O LORD, and lead me in a plain path, because of my enemies.* **Ps 27:11**
>
> *My little children, I am writing these things to you so that you may not sin. But if anyone does sin, we have an advocate with the Father, Jesus Christ the righteous.* **1 Jn 2:1**

Embark on this journey, venture through what it unveils. Receive, anticipating the manifestation in a manner similar to stating where you will go although you have yet to do so. It's not just looking to see; it's believing it to be. Continue reaching answers.

REACHING ANSWERS

Normally when we hear RA {sounds like rah!} there seems to be some cheering going on.

> O COME, let us sing unto the LORD: let us **make a joyful noise** to the rock of our salvation. Let us come before his presence with thanksgiving, and **make a joyful noise** unto him with psalms. **Ps 95:1-2**

There is joy in reaching answers that you need and want. You may experience a time no one is around that has answers. The path is not clear where to turn or to whom. Your walk is not self-directed although you are the one moving; if you are a believing child of God in Christ rooted in love.

My God, in Jesus' name I can't but only you can.

Answer everything with the Word of GOD! *If you can see the answer, you can reach it.*

I am faithfully in Christ ~ Eph 1 - 2. By faith I receive the greatest gift that could ever be given.

> Even before he made the world, God loved us and chose us in Christ to be holy and without fault in his eyes. God decided in advance to adopt us into his own family by bringing us to himself through Jesus Christ. This is what he wanted to do, and it gave him great pleasure. **Eph 1:4-5**

READ PSALMS 119 ~ A LOUD. It expounds on a believer's

experience.

Accepting the Lord Jesus Christ as your personal Saviour, resting in God's Word, covers a multitude of guiding commandments and statutes. This Psalms provides details for understanding the enhancement God seeks through you.

> *So then faith cometh* **by hearing,** *and* **hearing by** *the word of God.* **Ro 10:17**

Reading aloud constitutes hearing what is read. A believer should endeavor to align to God's Word.

Knowing who you are in Christ will keep you humble. This gives you the proper spirit to receive as well. Not every answer you reach will necessarily be the one you want to get.

When trials seem severe or things at their worse ~ encourage yourself.

> *And David was greatly distressed; for the people spake of stoning him, because the soul of all the people was grieved, every man for his sons and for his daughters: but David encouraged himself in the LORD his God.* **1 Sam 30:6**

Though David grieved as well as the people, they could not see his feelings being caught up in their own that they felt he brought upon them. Challenges will always exist in one form or another. Always do your best. Follow as the Holy Spirit leads unwaveringly believe - no matter what - you will succeed. Should you not quite reach the top, keep going anyhow - don't stop.

Yield unto the Holy Spirit to hear and receive divine guidance. He is the Comforter; living up to the divine designation if you trust

Him. He'll work within to work through every matter.

> *Nevertheless, I tell you the truth; It is expedient for you that I go away: for if I go not away, the Comforter will not come unto you; but if I depart, I will send him unto you.* And when he is come, he will reprove the world of sin, and of righteousness, and of judgment: Of sin, because they believe not on me; Of righteousness, because I go to my Father, and ye see me no more; Of judgment, because the prince of this world is judged. I have yet many things to say unto you, but ye cannot bear them now. Howbeit when he, the Spirit of truth, is come, he will guide you into all truth: for he shall not speak of *himself; but whatsoever he shall hear, that shall he speak: and he will shew you things to come.* He shall glorify me: for he shall *receive of mine, and shall shew it unto you.* All things that the Father hath are mine: therefore said I, that he shall take of mine, *and shall shew it unto you.* Jn 16:7-15

- Commit 1 to 3 days to pray **only** about receiving the wisdom of God ~ to be and remain in possession of what you seek!

- Speak in your heavenly language of tongues about the plan He provides to continually be in the desired state aligned to His will.

- For he that speaketh in an *unknown* tongue speaketh not unto men, but unto God: for no man understandeth ***him***; howbeit in the spirit he speaketh mysteries. **1 Cor 14:2**

- Pray until you know exactly what He has for you to do

- Decree the Lord's favour empoweringly anoints and enlarges your sphere of influence drawing more unto thee.

Lay a foundation that spiritually opens you to receive an answer. Reach in humility. Accept with respect and appreciation the answers you reach. Modifications to the answer(s) may be possible or reassessment might be necessary for what you truly seek. **Victory Principles** *are available to apply to various situations*: pray plant praise.

My victory comes when I _____ for it! What word completes this statement for you?

- What I need is not where I am; it's in another dimension and I must reach to reel it in!

- Urges deplete; instincts deposit

- Invest in what you influence

- Invest in what/whomever invests in you

- You can only set trends when you're not traceable /predictable

Stop thinking about what you are unable to do. Invest in options that can perform for you. Faithfully moving forward gains ground rather than fearfully standing still and being bound. If you already had the answers, you wouldn't be reaching, would you?

When you sow consider doing so in good, fertile soil. As an investment intended to garner a fruitful harvest, take care which ground you choose. Designate an identity for the seed based on the harvest you would like to reap. Sow a seed to reach the answer that addresses what you need. A few sample passages to identify your seeds accordingly to plant in good soil, are among these given below.

> *(The Lord God of your fathers make you a thousand times so many more as ye **are**, and bless you, as he hath promised you!)* **Deut 1:11**
>
> **But other fell into good ground, and brought forth fruit, some a hundredfold, some sixtyfold, some thirtyfold.** Mt 13:8
>
> ***I pray that** the eyes of your heart may be enlightened, ... Now unto him that is able to do exceedingly abundantly above all that we ask or think, according to the power that worketh in us...* **Eph 1:18a** and **Eph 3:20**
>
> Then Isaac sowed in that land, and received in the same year a hundredfold: and the Lord blessed him. **Gen 26:12**
>
> *For the seed **shall be** prosperous; the vine shall give her fruit, and the ground shall give her increase, and the heavens shall give their dew; and I will cause the remnant of this people to possess all these **things**.* **Zech 8:12**

> *He that receiveth a prophet in the name of a prophet shall receive a prophet's reward; and he that receiveth a righteous man in the name of a righteous man shall receive a righteous man's reward.* Mt 10:41 {prophet's reward}

And every one that hath forsaken houses, or brethren, or sisters, or father, or mother, or wife, or children, or lands, for my name's sake, shall receive an hundredfold, and shall inherit everlasting life. Mt 19:29

> *And Jesus answered and said,* **Verily I say unto you, There is no man that hath left house, or brethren, or sisters, or father, or mother, or wife, or children, or lands, for my sake, and the gospel's, But he shall receive an hundredfold now in this time, houses, and brethren, and sisters, and mothers, and children, and lands, with persecutions; and in the world to come eternal life.** Mk 10:29-30

> *The righteous shall flourish like the palm tree: he shall grow like a cedar in Lebanon.* Ps 92:12

The Lord shall command the blessing upon thee in thy storehouses, and in all that thou settest thine hand unto; and he shall bless thee in the land which the Lord thy God giveth thee.

> *The Lord shall open unto thee his good treasure, the heaven to give the rain unto thy land in his season, and to bless all the work of thine hand: and thou shalt lend unto many nations, and thou shalt not borrow.* **Deut 28:8 and** Deut 28:12 {blessings and good

treasure}

*Now he that ministereth seed to the sower both minister bread for **your** food, and multiply your seed sown, and increase the fruits of your righteousness;)* **2 Cor 9:10** *~ He multiplies seed sown giving thanks*

Owe no man anything, but to love one another: for he that loveth another hath fulfilled the law. **Ro 13:8** *~ Owe no man.*

Give, and it shall be given unto you; good measure, pressed down, and shaken together, and running over, shall men give into your bosom. For with the same measure that ye mete withal it shall be measured to you again. **Lk 6:38** *~ Same measure ye mete {6=connection; 3=resurrection; 8=new beginning}*

Honour the Lord with thy substance, and with the firstfruits of all thine increase: So shall thy barns be filled with plenty, and thy presses shall burst out with new wine. **Prv 3:9-10** *~ Firstfruits*

*Wealth and riches **shall be** in his house: and his righteousness endureth forever.* **Ps 112:3** *~ Wealth & riches & righteousness*

Decide what fits the occasion for the seed that is to be sown. Plant as needful. Plant as desired. Annotate your offering seed accordingly. Your harvest will not necessarily be in like kind ~ seed for seed. The product far outweighs the seed; just as an acorn produces a tree.

Apostle Paul's epistles ~ identify all we are **in Christ**. As a Pharisee, he governed in accordance with the Mosaic Law. His great knowledge, learning, and religious status secured him written authority to hunt and kill Christians. On the Damascus Road Jesus Christ blinded him to that charge converting him into a Christian with the gospel of good news for all receivers.

That changed! Can you imagine the drastically dramatic change unveiled in Apostle Paul's testimonial epistles? Read them to become familiar with the characteristics attributable to a Christian believer.

> *Study to shew thyself approved unto God, a workman that needeth not to be ashamed, rightly dividing the word of truth.* **2 Tim 2:15**

At least half of the 27 New Testament books are attributed to him. Those included are Romans, I and II Corinthians, Galatians, Ephesians, Philippians, Colossians, Philemon, I and II Thessalonians, I and II Timothy, Titus, and Hebrews. Of these, 7 are considered entirely authentic while others are disputed or questioned as being Paul's writing.

Reaching answers often invoke others speaking into or upon your life. Be careful what you allow to enter ~ by any means. This includes television, radio, environment, family, and/or friends.

Prophet/ess ~ forth (not fore) tells; represents; declares; announces God's will; carries oracles; reiterates promises; gives assurances; corrects; warns of the Messiah's presence (even forthcoming). Their telling is not of their own cognition. It is of divine discerning by the leading of the Holy Spirit of God. Take care in saying or hearing "God said". The Spirit of the Lord will confirm what aligns to His Word.

Key elements keep your will in alignment with God's directives.

- Goal: task oriented & limited

- Vision: ongoing & limitless ~ vital for achievements

These elements remain, even when it is necessary to modify them as you mature. Your audience and environment may prompt modifications as well.

> *That the God of our Lord Jesus Christ, the Father of glory, may give unto you the spirit of wisdom and revelation in the knowledge of him: The eyes of your understanding being **enlightened**; that ye may know what is the hope of his calling, and what the riches of the glory of his inheritance in the saints,...*
> **Eph 1:17-18**

GOD, Jesus Christ & the Holy Spirit live within me ~ going where I go coming against everything that comes against me! My endeavor is to do the Father's Will; among, about, unto all. I am to reflect His characteristics.

Seek ye first to know the instructional directives that you need to follow. You need to know where to go to determine a path to get there. It also helps you assess an encounter that prompts a detour or disruption to achieve your directive.

> *But seek ye first the kingdom of God, and his*

> *righteousness; and all these things shall be added unto you.* Mt 6:33

Ask for wisdom *(no matter what the need).* Seek wisdom to understand, to know when to go, where to go or whether to go at all. The wisdom of God excels your mere knowledge and may move you even though you have no idea where it's leading you.

> *If any of you lack wisdom, let him ask of God, that giveth to all **men** liberally, and upbraideth not; and it shall be given him. But let him ask in faith, nothing wavering. For he that wavereth is like a wave of the sea driven with the wind and tossed.* Jas 1:5-6

Have a little talk with Jesus. You don't always have to talk at all. He knows.

> *Likewise the Spirit also helpeth our infirmities: for we know not what we should pray for as we ought: but the Spirit itself maketh intercession for us with groanings which cannot **be uttered**.* Ro 8:26

> *And it shall come to pass, that before they call, I will answer; and while they are yet speaking, I will hear.* Is 65:24

His Spirit will guide you, especially when you are not sure how to phrase what you may need to ask! Follow as He leads to the answer you need to reach. He already knows the question and has the answer. He merely wants confirmation that you are aware it is Him you need.

In reaching answers towards fulfillment involves incorporating a prayer life. Prayer is talking with God. Remember, He's omniscient. He knows all therefore elements of subtlety or deceit have no place in this conversation or even your thoughts! {Not that you would entertain such things!}

Your prayers are that you be kept on a righteous path. Pray that you are surrounded by those that speak and impart into your life with honesty and integrity. Pray that mentors and influencers function with divine righteousness even if they do not believe or have faith in the God you serve.

Not all avenues lead you the way you should go nor are they borne of the same household. Not everyone believes the same, lives the same, or have all things in common. Differences do not negate the opportunities to contribute toward your answer in some way. If someone pays you for work that you perform; it is quite doubtful you would stop them to ask what they believe before accepting where the pay is coming from. Pray the provision is what the Lord would have you receive.

Pray to be kept while you are waiting for an answer. Pray that the answer is the one you truly need. Pray to stay committed to walking and moving righteously if reaching the finality of your answer appears to take a long, winding scenic route.

> *That ye might walk worthy of the Lord unto all pleasing, being fruitful in every good work, and increasing in the knowledge of God; Strengthened with all might, according to his glorious power, unto all patience and longsuffering with joyfulness;*
> **Col 1:10-11**

Pray, honoring God as supreme. Recognize His worthiness. Call the Lord, our Saviour My sufficiency, my matchless all in all!

Talk to the Lord when you arise. Bid Him to invoke His peace upon you so you can rest in Him throughout the night. As you talk with Him

- Honour Him
- Implore His will
- Request divine impartation of His Spirit
- Seek divine discernment
- Forgive
- Seek His forgiveness
- Move to forgiveness
- Lead, guide and deliver others by presenting the Word of God in faith
- Seek Thy kingdom's reign
- Align with Him more closely
- Thank Him for enemies that strengthened your resolve to stay in His Word and will
- Thank Him for keeping your mind, heart, and soul in His peace

Reaching out to God, our Father through our Saviour ~ Jesus Christ is not a coping mechanism; it is life's substance! Let your life reflect His kingdom. Let your reflection show you reaching answers. Take no offence when anyone throws shade upon your light.

> **THERE** is therefore now no condemnation to them which are in Christ Jesus, who walk not after the flesh, but after the Spirit. **Ro 8:1**

Great peace have they which love thy law and nothing shall offend them. **Ps 119:165**

And the light shineth in darkness; and the darkness comprehended it not. **Jo 1:5**

*The heart of him that hath understanding seeketh knowledge: but the mouth of fools feedeth on **foolishness**.* **Prv 15:14**

You cannot know or understand what can only be spiritually discerned. Religion does not have domain in this arena. Seek God in Christ for reaching answers.

Seeds are sown, deliberately planted with purpose. Weeds just grow ~ disrupts fruitfulness.

"Thinking is the real work. Think solution**s**. Bind negativity and contrariness to the Word of God." **Min David Ibiyeomi**

*Finally, brethren, whatsoever things **are** true, whatsoever things **are** honest, whatsoever things **are** just, whatsoever things **are** pure, whatsoever things **are** lovely, whatsoever things **are** of good report; if **there be** any virtue, and if **there be** any praise, think on these things.* **Phil 4: 8**

For as he thinketh in his heart, so is he:... **Prv 23:7a-b**

Prayer ~ draws God to a region

Praise ~ marks the spot for honor and glory to reign

A seed can only grow when planted in fertile soil greater than its own size. Plant purposefully. Nurture lovingly. This includes a seed of prayer and/or a seed of praise. A harvest is the answer you are trying to reach.

> For the seed **shall be** prosperous; the vine shall give her fruit, and the ground shall give her increase, and the heavens shall give their dew; and I will cause the remnant of this people to possess all these **things**.
> Zech 8:12

> Death and life **are** in the power of the tongue: and they that love it shall eat the fruit thereof.
> Prv 18:21

Speak to everything. Speak to the answers that you seek. Speak to the dilemmas that you meet. Believe what you speak in prayer at the moment of their rendering.

> **And Jesus answering saith unto them,** Have faith in God. For verily I say unto you, That whosoever shall say unto this mountain, Be thou removed, and be thou cast into the sea; and shall not doubt in his heart, but shall believe that those things which he saith shall come to pass; he shall have whatsoever he saith. Therefore, I say unto you, What things soever ye desire, when ye pray, believe that ye receive **them**, and ye shall have **them**. Mk 11:22-24

God wants us to **trust** Him. Trust His **Word** even without clearly understanding it. This requires believing faith. Hope evidenced by knowing even when you really don't know.

> NOW faith is the substance of things hoped for, the

> *evidence of things not seen.* **Heb 11:1**

Trust implies you can ASK. You feel you can rely on the one being asked. You believe the one being asked is able to help you reach your answer.

> *Ask, and it shall be given you; seek, and ye shall find; knock, and it shall be opened unto you: For every one that asketh receiveth; and he that seeketh findeth; and to him that knocketh it shall be opened.* **Mt 7:7-8**

> *Therefore let no man glory in men. For all things are yours;...* **1 Cor 3:21**

One quality that helps in reaching answers in places where it might appear that you can't is honoring thyself by keeping your word. Your word is still your bond. If what you say cannot be trusted, you cannot say anything worth trusting. No one would know which truth is the lie. There would be nothing you could say on which they could rely. Let a life of righteous integrity undergird whatsoever you speak. This will help the words that you speak and aid the answers you reach.

> *My mouth shall speak of wisdom; and **the meditation of my heart shall be** of understanding.* **Ps 49:3**

> ***The** secret of **the** Lord is with them that fear him; and he will shew them his covenant.* **Ps 25:14** ~ God will shew you His secret

God chose you before the foundation of this world. You are an honorable part of His kingdom reaching answers that draw others unto Him. He shall not forsake Himself by forsaking you.

> *According as he hath chosen us in him **before the***

*foundation of the world, that we should be holy and without blame **before** him in love:...* **Eph 1:4**

Nevertheless the foundation of God standeth sure, having this seal, The Lord knoweth them that are his. And, Let every one that nameth the name of Christ depart from iniquity. **2 Tim 2:19**

*But in a great house there are not only vessels of gold and of silver, but also of wood and of earth; and some to honour, and some to dishonour. If a man therefore purge himself from these, he shall be a vessel unto honour, sanctified, and meet for the master's use, **and** prepared unto every good work.* **2 Tim 2:20-21**

As a representative for God in Christ reaching answers is necessary to provide a just model. Those among you that are lost in circumstances, mental issues, and life's chances need a vessel of honor to shed light in their dark places. God does not need fleshly depictions perpetrating holy righteousness that lacks quality.

Exercise your spiritual senses ~ communicate; meditate; pray; study the Word; worship. These tools help you in reaching answers. They help discern if what is presented to you will lead to what you need it to. Your spiritual senses open you:

- To hear God more clearly and regularly than other voices or **noise -** *even from yourself*

- accept your **own worthiness** in places you may feel unworthy; wherever you may feel out of place - get rooted; ***don't run!***

- Learn from what you don't know, especially from environments you're not sure you belong

- share what you know whether you feel it is being received or not ~ plant - all soil is not fertile

- remodel your life with things and people that feed you - feed your spirit!

- advance toward your destiny - celebrate **you**

- so you can always connect with those that need you; even some that you have to wean in the process

Reaching answers may sound like an easy thing to do. Challenges come in many forms from various avenues too. Be certain that this is not a self-sufficient process. The Lord needs you to be your best you, open to His leading in order to receive what He has for you.

Reaching answers may not be merely needed for yourself. You may need those very answers to be a light within reach for someone else. Some that do not know the Lord are reaching too. If perhaps they cross paths with you will a light of understanding shine through?

He will answer. Will you receive? Be open to trusting Him by faith. Do you believe? Be purposeful in aligning to His Holy Spirit to do all you can toward reaching answers designed just for you.

Once you accept the Word of God as truth and receive Jesus Christ as your divine Lord and Saviour, a blessed assurance envelope you. You learn to recognize that God presents declarations in His Word. The states given manifest whether suddenly or over time, providing completion of the inherent process.

*For this God **is** our God for ever and ever: he will be*

> *our guide even unto death.* **Ps 48:14**

> *Let not your heart be troubled: ye believe in God, believe also in me.* **Jn 14:1**

> *Ye **are** my witnesses, saith the Lord, and my servant whom I have chosen: that ye may know and believe me, and understand that I **am** he: before me there was no God formed, neither shall there be after me.* **Is 43:10**

Your understanding of things experienced deepens as guided by the Holy Spirit of God. Your witness intensifies.

The sincerity of your faith is not fleeting although it may be challenged. Knowing the reliability of God's Word helps you stand faithfully if waiting is needful rather than trying to make things happen yourself. Since faith comes by hearing, speak what the Word says to hear what it is telling you and believe it.

> *So then faith cometh* **by hearing**, *and* **hearing by** *the word of God.* **Ro 10:17**

> *But without faith it is impossible to please him: for he that cometh to God must believe that he is, and that he is a rewarder of them that diligently seek him.* **Heb 11:6**

Perhaps a petition in the form of a spiritual check to cash is needed. If you trust the source, will you bank on its truth? Just to add a bit more flavor a few examples follow to stand on, speak on, and rely on as true. Some of the resources from which the petition may be drawn follow the checks given.

```
Mount Sion, Eternity
                                              Requested _____  Date ____
Pay to the Order of _____ RECIPIENT _____  ∞
_____ Discernment and/or Prophesy _____
For :_Needs to be met continually_           JEHOVAH-El Roi
```

```
Mount Sion, Eternity
                                              Requested _____  Date ____
Pay to the Order of _____ RECIPIENT _____  ∞
_____ Family _____
For :_Needs to be met continually_           JEHOVAH-Mekaddishkem
```

```
Mount Sion, Eternity
                                              Requested _____  Date ____
Pay to the Order of _____ RECIPIENT _____  ∞
_____ Fear _____
For :_Needs to be met continually_           JEHOVAH-Elohe Yeshuathi
```

```
Mount Sion, Eternity
                                              Requested _____  Date ____
Pay to the Order of _____ RECIPIENT _____  ∞
_____ Salvation _____
For :_Needs to be met continually_           JEHOVAH- Keren-Yishi
```

JEHOVAH-El Roi - the God Who Sees [Gen 16:13]

And she called the name of the Lord that spake unto her, Thou God seest me: for she said, Have I also here looked after him that seeth me? **Genesis 16:13**

Whoso keepeth the commandment shall feel no evil thing: and a wise man's heart discerneth both time and judgment. **Ecclesiastes 8:5**

But he that prophesieth speaketh unto men to edification, and exhortation, and comfort. **1 Corinthians 14:3**

JEHOVAH-Mekaddishkem - the Lord Who Sanctifies You [Exodus 31:13]

Speak thou also unto the children of Israel, saying, Verily my sabbaths ye shall keep: for it *is* a sign between me and you throughout your generations; that *ye* may know that I *am* the Lord that doth sanctify you. **Exodus 31:13**

And *that ye* will save alive my father, and my mother, and my brethren, and my sisters, and all that they have, and deliver our lives from death. **Joshua 2:13**

...Choose you this day whom ye will serve;... but as for me and my house, we will serve the Lord. **Joshua 24:15b, f & g**

JEHOVAH-Elohe Yeshuathi - the God of My Salvation [Psalms 88:1]

O Lord God of *my* salvation, I have cried day *and* night before thee:... **Psalms 88:1**

I sought the Lord, and he heard me, and delivered me from all my fears. **Psalms 34:4**

For ye have not received the spirit of bondage again to fear; but ye have received the Spirit of adoption, whereby we cry, Abba, Father. **Romans 8:15**

For God hath not given us the spirit of fear; but of power, and of love, and of a sound mind. **2 Timothy 1:7**

JEHOVAH- Keren-Yishi - the Lord the Horn of My Salvation [Psalms 18:2]

The Lord *is* my rock, and my fortress, and my deliverer; my God, my strength, in whom I will trust; my buckler, and the horn of my salvation, *and* my high tower. **Psalms 18:2**

Thus saith the Lord, Keep ye judgment, and do justice: for my salvation *is* near to come, and my righteousness to be revealed. **Isaiah 56:1**

Whoso offereth praise glorifieth me: and to him that ordereth *his* conversation *aright* will I shew the salvation of God. **Psalms 50:23**

If those do not quite meet the need here are a few more spiritual checks for you. Perhaps these will provide what you need them to. Potential resources for them follow as well.

```
Mount Sion, Eternity
                                    _____ Requested _____ Date
Pay to the Order of _____ RECIPIENT _____ ∞
_____ Health _____
For : _Needs to be met continually_        JEHOVAH - Raphe/Rophe
```

```
Mount Sion, Eternity
                                    _____ Requested _____ Date
Pay to the Order of _____ RECIPIENT _____ ∞
_____ Prosperity _____
For : _Needs to be met continually_              JEHOVAH - Jireh
```

```
Mount Sion, Eternity
                                    _____ Requested _____ Date
Pay to the Order of _____ RECIPIENT _____ ∞
_____ Whatever you need just ask _____
For : _Needs to be met continually_                     JESUS
```

```
Mount Sion, Eternity
                                    _____ Requested _____ Date
Pay to the Order of _____ RECIPIENT _____ ∞
_____ Wisdom _____
For : _Needs to be met continually_                JEHOVAH - Ori
```

JEHOVAH - Raphe/Rophe - the Lord that Heals {Exodus 15:26}

A merry heart doeth good *like* a medicine: but a broken spirit drieth the bones. **Prov 17:22**

My son, attend to my words; incline thine ear unto my sayings. Let them not depart from thine eyes; keep them in the midst of thine heart. For they *are* life unto those that find them, and health to all their flesh. **Proverbs 4:20-22**

And said, If thou wilt diligently hearken to the voice of the Lord thy God, and wilt do that which is right in his sight, and wilt give ear to his commandments, and keep all his statutes, I will put none of these diseases upon thee, which I have brought upon the Egyptians: for I *am* the Lord that healeth thee. **Exodus 15:26**

JEHOVAH - Jireh -- the Lord Will Provide - [Genesis 22:14]

This book of the law shall not depart out of thy mouth; but thou shalt meditate therein day and night, that thou mayest observe to do according to all that is written therein: for then thou shalt make thy way prosperous, and then thou shalt have good success. **Joshua 1:8**

Beloved, I wish above all things that thou mayest prosper and be in health, even as thy soul prospereth. **3 John 1:2**

Peace be within thy walls, *and* prosperity within thy palaces. **Psalms 122:7**

JESUS

If ye abide in me, and my words abide in you, ye shall ask what ye will, and it shall be done unto you. **John 15:7**

And this is the confidence that we have in him, that, if we ask any thing according to his will, he heareth us: And if we know that he hear us, whatsoever we ask, we know that we have the petitions that we desired of him. **1 John 5:14-15**

JEHOVAH - Ori - the Lord My Light {Psalms 27:1}

Teach me thy way, O Lord, and lead me in a plain path, because of mine enemies. **Psalms 27:11**

The Lord *is* my light and my salvation; whom shall I fear? the Lord *is* the strength of my life; of whom shall I be afraid? **Psalms 27:1**

Of course, these are merely examples of what standing on the Word or God entails."

Be careful when petitioning God. His answers are not always received. When the answer wanted does not come as desired or sometimes comes as asked, the enemy can blind you with doubt or merely disbelief.

If you're reaching, God will answer ~ have no doubt. Will you trust His response? Cash in a spiritual check and find out!

It's not so monumental to know how God will answer; it's crucial to openly and receptively listen attentively to respond promptly when He does.

REFERENCES

Scriptures referenced throughout Reaching Answers are from the King James Version; Message Version; English Standard Version; New American Standard Bible; and/or New Living Translation of the Holy Bible.

DIVINE BOUNDARIES

Reaching for answers is worth the expended effort.

My prayer is your journey through these pages unveiled a few avenues towards fulfillment.

www.ingramcontent.com/pod-product-compliance
Lightning Source LLC
Chambersburg PA
CBHW041215130526
44582CB00024BA/3